Becoming a 1

Guide to becoming the best
background actor

Contents

Introduction

From someone being involved in over a hundred movie sets through the course of a year to landing my first speaking role I have learned the process in doing so. I got to have one of the best years of my life with meeting and hanging out with crew, BG, and a few stand-ins who pursue acting to the fullest. There is no secret movie magic is real and you will see what it means to be a part of something with hundreds of different people creating something viewed by millions. Entertaining people is the way of life for many of us as we make a career being featured in the background or standing in for the main actors.

Growing from background acting to speaking roles has been an exciting challenge. I have been able to form long lasting relationships and friendships with the people I have met on set. There is nothing more special than being around people who share similar interests and goals in this magical industry.

There are many different crew members responsible for tasks from operating the dolly, controlling lighting and positioning the camera to make sure the scene is perfect. Usually pa's will walk around with waters and snacks as they understand having happy background performers is as important as having happy actors.

When I took my first step on a movie set there was hunger in my heart to be noticed by the camera and everyone there. I ended up landing more projects than I can count from working stand in, photo doubling and background work. To be clear I was also managing five classes a semester while having a social life so it is definitely possible to make a career background acting while pursuing your other desires. The best thing about this type of work is that you get to pick the roles and dates you are available. There will be many opportunities for you to succeed in this industry and possibly meet some famous celebrities along the way.

Headshots and Audition Reels

Above is an example of a perfectly fine headshot to use when applying for roles.

Here is an example of one not as good. The model in the photo is great but casting directors do not like to see a lot going on in the background and just like seeing your pretty face.

Getting a good headshot is important but not as important as having originality. Casting directors like uniqueness, before I had professional headshots I made it on plenty of sets with just regular old selfies. You can always use Photoshop or editing apps on your phone as well to create a better headshot without having to spend money you don't have. Casting directors get thousands of emails a day and if you look unique they will take note regardless of the expensive headshot.

Next piece of advice to landing a role especially one that requires an audition is through an audition video. Try to create a demo reel or a specific video to the role known as the audition reel. You can do this yourself by placing your camera in a position where it's aimed at you or by having a friend record you.

A good video is important because the people casting the role in which you are submitting want to see that you have what it takes in order to pull off the character's emotions and look. Try buying props to be placed in the background or used by you in which the character might have. If it is the 1980's and the character you are auditioning for is a rocker type then maybe have a Guns N' Roses poster in the background, something that pertains to the time and character. Directors will narrow down their choices between headshots, demo reels, examining the camera presence, style and versatility that the actor comes into the shot with. Your acting must be impressive enough to land the role so taking many shots and some minor acting classes can be the biggest difference in landing the role or not. Background roles usually never require an audition reel though. Take your time in developing good selfies or professional headshots to use and remember the ones that receive responses for projects as those are the ones you should keep submitting.

Where to submit

Background acting is easy to get into once you know where to submit.

Here are some websites, emails and phone numbers that will get you on the right track to apply.

Websites

www.projectcasting.com - This free casting site has the most popular new movies and television series to apply for from Marvel's Avenger's movies to The Walking Dead. It includes all the emails to apply to.

www.NYCasting.com - This New York based casting company allows you to submit for commercial, print, voice-over and background roles.

www.Backstage.com - This site has small, medium and large projects. It is a premium site that costs around $12 a month but is very reliable with great feedback of landing jobs.

www.ActorsAccess.com - On actors access you will showcase your skills. You will submit your talent through resumes, videos and pictures so casting directors can see your unique look and skills.

www.TheSoutherncCastingcall.com - Includes popular agencies that are hiring for projects in the south.

Emails and phone numbers

[CentralCasting]

Central is one of the largest casting agencies in the world and has employed thousands of people. They have different emails to apply to for the many projects they cast so look on their Facebook page, one for example is macatl@centralcasting.com

Phone number- (404) 920-8011
Give them a call and they will help you.

[Rose Locke Casting]

Rose Locke Casting does a lot of casting as well and will post on their Facebook page all the time for background and stand in positions. Their email is Extras@roselockecasting.com

{Catrett Locke Casting]

Catrett Locke Casting is similar to Rose Locke except their email is Submissions@Catrettcasting.com

[Marinella Hume Casting]

Marinella does a lot of casting for younger types and also does casting for music videos, they are very responsive. They use different emails for the many projects they are casting for, one for example is mhc.originals@gmail.com

[ECA]

Extras Casting Atlanta is a big casting agency that casts comedy genres, horrors and just about any film in Atlanta. Their email is extrascastingtv@gmail.com

[Hylton Casting]

Hylton casting casts for commercials, court scenes and a variety of extra positions. Their email is audience@hyltoncasting.com

Phone number- (404) 936-1105

[Casting TaylorMade]

Casting Taylor Made connects background actors, performers and extras. Their email is extrascastingtm@gmail.com

[Tammy Smith Casting]

Tammy Smith casting casts for marvel movies and new hit television series. Their email is projects1@TSCasting.com

[Pierre Casting]

Pierre Casting is based in Atlanta, Georgia and is one of Atlanta's leading production companies. Their email is info@pierrecasting.com

Phone Number- (404) 551-7238

Overall a good place to start will be www.Backstage.com as you can enter your location and find jobs in your area that pertain to the type of work you're interested in but any of the websites will help guide you to this new fascinating job.

What to say in a casting email

Now that you have the agencies to apply to the next step is understanding how to apply.

If the project is asking for Asian or Caucasian men between the ages of 25 and 40 to submit that can pull off a detective look then make sure you are applying only if that applies to you.

In order to stand out you should have an appropriate email to use, maybe something that is eye popping to stand out from the hundreds of other applicants applying. When submitting for the role make sure you list your name, number, location and all your size requirements such as height, weight, pants, shirt and shoe size.

Create an email presence using friendly and exciting words to show you are happy to be applying, this works great when you have no experience to list. Adding a smile face or exclamation can go a long way. Casting directors want to know that you are someone approachable who will bring good energy to the set which will make them want to hire you.

Once you have been in the background game for a while you will notice agencies are emailing or texting you first and you don't even have to apply anymore.

That is what happened to me but let's say on the contrary they are not responding to you anymore you can always register a new email address and phone number and apply again.

The agencies you are emailing want to see creative, unique and polite emails. Personally having been a part of so many sets I learned the formula and after every email I include sincerely with my name. Being professional doesn't hurt as well and makes them know you take your job seriously.

Only apply for positions in which you match the requirements or this will irritate some casting directors.

Casting directors get flooded with emails from people who want to be in the movie industry constantly. Differentiating your email writing is the key difference in landing the role or losing it to someone else with a friendlier email presence. Follow these rules and you will be on your way to landing the role you want.

First rule in email submissions is following the submission guidelines. If the agency specifies you to send 2 headshots and one full length shot then send those required shots, you wouldn't believe the amount of times people don't get casted based on sending in the wrong photo requirements.

Second rule that has helped me in landing roles through email submissions is not being afraid to have fun. Many casting directors are bored seeing the same emails and love expression so don't be deterred from adding a smile face in the email or an exclamation as standing out from the pact and bringing an energetic personality is highly desired in the entertainment industry.

There are many tricks to email submissions. If you feel you have sent too many emails with bad headshots then change up your email address most casting directors will not even recognize the change in email, only the change in new headshots as they have to deal with thousands of potential background actors a day.

On set behavior

So you found the right agency, applied and alas you received your very own confirmation email that will include the time, date, wardrobe and location details of the day you are booked. This is exciting, you are beyond happy to tell all your friends and family that you are working on television, what else is cooler? Well now that you've made it you need to ensure that you stay involved. Having a great personality and being nice to the right people will ensure that you get call backs and emails for future projects. Remember no photos or atleast be secretive with it because you could get kicked off set.

Approaching the right people: My time working in the movie industry I have talked to producers, directors, actors, crew members and a variety of different background actors. Having meaningful conversations and networking, obtaining phone numbers, emails and communicating with these people has separated me from the countless extras.

You will get a sense of the right time to communicate with these people, when I did stand in work for main actors of projects I was able to consistently talk to them. Constantly I see too many times people reading on set, playing board games or goofing around when that is fun and all but at the end of the day being on set you should be networking and learning as much as you can about the set and people working on it as there is more information to be learned through networking than reading a book at this time. With that said, sometimes actors or crew are busy and do not have the time to talk to you, do not be offended as they have a job to do just like you. When you are on set take direction wisely, you will be placed and don't try to stand out too much as this can get the director irritated if you do. Another reason you may not want to stand out too much on camera is that you may not get called back if you have too much camera time even in the background. From someone who frequently gets placed next to main actors in scenes I know how it is done. You should try to speak with the AD (Assistant director) who is the one placing you when you think of something clever to say, funny or have an idea about the scene. These people love learning just as much as you do and typically won't get irritated if you have an idea on what you could do or have a conversation starter, in fact having a meaningful conversation with the right person will lead them to want you to come back and work with them on future projects. Now there are many things you should avoid when working on set such as alcohol, drugs and cigarettes. Crew on sets smoke like a chimney but unless you are specifically asked to smoke or drink don't do it, it doesn't look good for you and can make the set look trashy. I have seen too many times before when people got high and kicked off set, without pay because of it. If you do your job correctly, network politely and bring good energy to the set you will get call backs.

Rates and pay bumps

Now to the exciting part, money.
There is much money to be made doing background, stand in and photo double work if you do it consistently. Also remember you get fed lunch and crafty for free on every set.

Rates

The typical pay rate- 64, 68/8. That means you will receive a minimum of $64 even if you work less than 8 hours. There is also overtime which means after 8 hours of work you make extra money, typically $12 after every hour past 8 hours which adds up.

Pay rate for background occasionally 88/10

Pay rate for featured background 150/8

Pay rate for stand in 140/12

Pay rate for photo double 140/12

Bumps

Make sure to tell the PA at the end of the night, the person who signs you out that you should receive a pay bump if the following applies to you.

Prosthetic pay bump: When more than 50% of your body is covered in makeup and prosthetics you will receive a bump on your voucher.

Hair bump: When you get a drastic hair cut for photo double or background role you should typically receive from $10-75 bump plus a free haircut.

Car pay bump: Sometimes when applying for roles the agency will want you to use your car and a lot of the time you get to just sit in it for eight hours while making the same extra rate plus $25.

Water bump: When getting wet other than from the rain such as getting used in a pool or having water splashed on you, you should receive a $15 pay bump.

Smoke Bump: When required to smoke cigarettes you should receive a $15 bump.

Pet Bump: Whenever you are asked to bring in a pet to set you should be compensated $23 for it.

Meal Penalties

A Meal penalty is the amount of time you spent at lunch, which is typically 6 hours after crew call. Meal penalties will take time off of your voucher because let's face it, you are eating not working.

The meal penalty will usually deduct thirty minutes to an hour off of your money voucher but hey, free meals.

Important words to succeed on set

Now that you have made it on set you will want to understand the phrases and terms thrown out and used so frequently.
Terms that took me months to learn.

Continuity- Keeping consistent details in each scene of the film

Background Action- This is the term used when background is supposed to begin their actions.

Action- This is the term used when actors are supposed to begin their actions.

Rehearsals up- Practice to show what the scene will look like

Pictures up- Comes after rehearsals and means the film will be rolling on action.

2nd Team- The stand ins come to their marks, where the main actors will be

1st Team- When the main actors get to their marks and replace the stand ins.

Cut- Transition from one scene to the next, the stop of actions usually called out by the 1st AD.

AD- Assistant Director, usually in charge of directing background.

Martini shot- The last shot of filming for the day

Wrap- Every scene for the day is finished

Crew Call- Time that the crew gets to set

Back to your 1's- When someone says get to your 1's this means they want you in the previous position you were before lunch or before they yelled cut.

Crafty- This is the place where all the snacks, water or coffee is.

Checking the gate- After a successful shot the scene must be checked to see that there were no strips of film emulsion that may have come off.

Pantomime- When asked to pantomime this means you should move your lips as if you are talking but without projecting sound.

Copy that- You understand the direction given to you.

Call time- The time you are supposed to be on set, usually arrive 15-30 minutes prior to call time in case of unplanned traffic or to network.

Stand by- Stay in your positions to prepare for rolling.

Go again- Repeat the same action you previously did.

What's your 20? - Where are you positioned for the scene.

Lock it up- Be silent and ready for the cameras to start rolling.

"Thumbs up"- You did a perfect job.

Wardrobe Necessities

Many times on set there will be wardrobe options available to you especially when working with bigger agencies. However, even these agencies will still want you to bring fall, spring, winter or summer options determining on the scene. Most of the time you will be asked to bring sneakers, boots, shirts, jackets and black socks.

Having a variety of options to bring with you will make you look professional and if you get approved by costumes with your own clothes then you will not have to wait in the wardrobe line to get your voucher back because they will take your money voucher if you borrow their clothes. The next reason you should always bring your best wardrobe options is because it makes you look professional. Wearing your own clothes may make you feel more comfortable as well than wearing some clothes that may not have been washed in a while.

Having the right clothes on can be the difference in being placed closed to the actors or being placed deep in the background. If you have stylish clothes wear them, if your wardrobe is lacking good options still bring what you can as showing up on set with no options can actually get you kicked off. I have seen my friend forget to bring a costume and she was asked to leave without pay. Go shopping at goodwill with the wardrobe list and you will be surprised by the amount of clothes that you can find that are still stylish and will be acceptable for the scene. Strengthening your wardrobe options to wear can make the biggest difference in the entertainment world.

Believe in your craft

If you don't believe in your craft how are other supposed to? Tell your pals, excite your family and add your background jobs to your actor resume. Working in this industry can get tiring, the late nights and early call times exhaust even the hardest working people.

You should know that without your work in the movie there would be no movie. Without background artists like you to fill in the background of a 1970's or modern day film the movie wouldn't be the same.

Your friends who don't do extra work may not understand why you aren't hanging out as much or have to work strange hours of the day but your work does not go unnoticed.

People will recognize when you are on time, bring a friendly attitude and network. Your job helps the movie become the success that it is.
There are many actors who started out as background actors including Sylvester Stallone, Bruce Willis, Brad Pitt, Clint Eastwood, Megan Fox, James Dean, Marilyn Monroe and even Jackie Chan.

Just because your current job title may be an extra doesn't mean you can't move up in the world as an actor if you choose. Believing that your work has importance will help motivate you to want to succeed in this industry. Choose to care about your background job as the casting directors will take note of those who go the extra mile and will continue to book you on projects if you just believe in yourself and strive to be your best. Never let someone tell you that you are just an extra because you are more, you are an actor.

22294423R00016

Printed in Poland
by Amazon Fulfillment
Poland Sp. z o.o., Wrocław